SCHOLASTIC

GRADES
2–3

Solve & Match
Math Practice
PAGES

50+ Motivating, Self-Checking Activities That
Help Kids Review and Master Essential Math Skills

ERIC CHARLESWORTH

New York • Toronto • London • Auckland • Sydney **Teaching**
Mexico City • New Delhi • Hong Kong • Buenos Aires *Resources*

*To the faculty and staff at Paul Cuffee School, who are always busy inspiring kids,
but never so much that they can't stop for a moment to inspire me.*

—EC

Edited by Sarah Longhi
Cover design by Jason Robinson
Interior design by Melinda Belter

ISBN: 978-0-545-28815-6

Copyright © 2011 by Eric Charlesworth
All rights reserved. Printed in the U.S.A.

1 2 3 4 5 6 7 8 9 10   40   18 17 16 15 14 13 12 11

CONTENTS

INTRODUCTION

If you've been looking for easy new ways to motivate your students to build and practice important math skills, this book of 50+ reproducible pages is for you.

Sure, students can benefit from practicing skills on their own. But independent practice often provides little support, leaving students who are unsure of their skills without guidance and even reinforcing bad habits when students repeat mistakes. The Solve & Match format was designed to overcome these pitfalls of independent work.

While students are solving the problems on these practice pages, they will be able to verify each answer by finding a matching answer on the page. If answers are not matching up, then students will quickly discover where their mistakes may be—and fix them on the spot. And when answers are matching up, students experience the satisfaction of knowing they are *getting it*!

When I began using the Solve & Match format for homework, the payoffs were clear from the beginning. Students began to:

• catch and fix their own mistakes

• stop skipping problems

• report that this type of homework was fun and ask for more!

The activities in this book have been aligned to the Common Core State Standards, and the contents are divided into easy-to-navigate sections. The reproducible format clearly lends itself well to homework assignments but can also be used for class warm-ups, morning work, or fun practice for fast finishers.

Some other features of interest in this book include the following:

Bonus challenge problems Each page features a "Triple Match Challenge," which offers students a more difficult problem to solve. The answer to this problem will match up with two other answers on the page, so students can check their work.

Word problems Several pages provide problem-solving practice with words. Students get to take their new skills to the zoo, the mall, and the construction site, where they will face authentic story problems.

I hope these activities provide new options for the review and practice of essential math skills. And I hope your students not only enjoy the Solve & Match format but gain confidence as they take charge of their learning and sharpen their skills!

Name _____   Date _____

Finding Patterns I

Find the missing number. Draw a line to match each answer on the left with one on the right.

LEFT

1. 1, 4, 7, _____

2. 10, 20, _____, 40

3. 6, _____, 18, 24

4. _____, 10, 15, 20

5. 36, 38, _____, 42

6. 100, 200, 300, _____

RIGHT

A. 3, 6, 9, _____

B. 200, _____, 600, 800

C. 2, 6, _____, 14

D. 2, 3, 4, _____

E. 20, _____, 60, 80

F. 15, 20, 25, _____

TRIPLE MATCH Challenge

Complete this number pattern: 72, 52, 32, _____

Circle the answers that match above.

Name _____ Date _____

Finding Patterns II

Find the missing number. Draw a line to match each answer on the left with one on the right.

LEFT   **RIGHT**

1. 100, 75, _____ , 25   **A.** 33, 23, 13, _____

2. 29, _____ , 37, 41   **B.** 11, 22, _____ , 44

3. 10, 8, 6, _____   **C.** 30, 40, 50, _____

4. 44, 32, 20, _____   **D.** 200, 150, 100, _____

5. 15, 30, 45, _____   **E.** 6, 7, _____ , 9

6. 9, 7, 5, _____   **F.** 0, _____ , 8, 12

TRIPLE MATCH Challenge

A pattern starts with 16 and decreases by 2 with each number. What is the fifth number of the sequence? _____

Circle the answers that match above.

Solve & Match Math Practice Pages: Grades 2–3 © 2011 Eric Charlesworth, Scholastic Teaching Resources

Name _____   Date _____

Comparing Numbers

Solve each problem. Draw a line to match each answer on the left with one on the right.

LEFT   **RIGHT**

1. 10 greater than 6 =   **A.** 6 greater than 10 =

2. 7 less than 9 =   **B.** 10 less than 24 =

3. 6 less than 20 =   **C.** 8 less than 10 =

4. 14 less than 20 =   **D.** 10 greater than 14 =

5. 5 greater than 10 =   **E.** 6 greater than 9 =

6. 12 greater than 12 =   **F.** 6 less than 12 =

TRIPLE MATCH Challenge

An odd number is greater than 13 and less than 17. What number is it? _____

Circle the answers that match above.

Name _____   Date _____

Identifying Place Value

For each number, name the place value of the 5. Draw a line to match each answer on the left with one on the right.

| ones   tens   hundreds |
| thousands   ten thousands |
| hundred thousands   millions |

LEFT

1. 152,764

_____

2. 315

_____

3. 35,671

_____

4. 514,098

_____

5. 452

_____

6. 24,570

_____

RIGHT

A. 4,315

_____

B. 1,567,093

_____

C. 3,500

_____

D. 14,659

_____

E. 51,000

_____

F. 875,640

_____

TRIPLE MATCH Challenge

In the number 371,291, which place value has an even digit?

_____

Circle the answers that match above.

Solve & Match Math Practice Pages: Grades 2–3 © 2011 Eric Charlesworth, Scholastic Teaching Resources

Name _____ Date _____

Ordering Numbers

In each number set, circle the **highest** number. Draw a line to match each answer on the left with one on the right.

LEFT	**RIGHT**
1. 114, 112, 117, 19	**A.** 117, 147, 144, 150
2. 120, 150, 55, 119	**B.** 65, 155, 100, 152
3. 133, 137, 131, 130	**C.** 134, 139, 145, 78
4. 190, 109, 191, 19	**D.** 117, 109, 107, 114
5. 150, 130, 133, 155	**E.** 99, 191, 189, 150
6. 144, 142, 145, 136	**F.** 117, 127, 137, 135

TRIPLE MATCH Challenge

In a fishing tournament, Hank caught 137 fish, Oscar caught 155 fish, and Owen caught 117 fish. What is the LEAST number of fish that someone caught? _____

Circle the answers that match above.

Name _____   Date _____

Doubling, Tripling, Quadrupling

Find each answer. Draw a line to match each answer on the left with one on the right.

LEFT	RIGHT
What is . . .	**What is . . .**

1. double the number 6? _____   **A.** double the number 9? _____

2. triple the number 6? _____   **B.** double the number 10? _____

3. quadruple the number 6? _____   **C.** quadruple the number 3? _____

4. triple the number 10? _____   **D.** double the number 12? _____

5. quadruple the number 5? _____   **E.** triple the number 2? _____

6. double the number 3? _____   **F.** double the number 15? _____

TRIPLE MATCH Challenge

Take the number 2 and triple it. Take that answer and double it. Now take that answer and double it. What did you get? _____

Circle the answers that match above.

Solve & Match Math Practice Pages: Grades 2–3 © 2011 Eric Charlesworth, Scholastic Teaching Resources

Name _____   Date _____

Rounding to Tens

Round each value to the nearest ten. Draw a line to match each answer on the left with one on the right.

LEFT   **RIGHT**

1. 18 = _____   **A.** 74 = _____

2. 31 = _____   **B.** 88 = _____

3. 14 = _____   **C.** 15 = _____

4. 65 = _____   **D.** 53 = _____

5. 47 = _____   **E.** 8 = _____

6. 91 = _____   **F.** 26 = _____

TRIPLE MATCH Challenge

Round the answer of 9×8 to the nearest ten. _____

Circle the answers that match above.

Name _____   Date _____

Rounding to Hundreds

Round each value to the nearest hundred. Draw a line to match each answer on the left with one on the right.

LEFT   **RIGHT**

1. 671 =   **A.** 90 =

2. 455 =   **B.** 350 =

3. 320 =   **C.** 818 =

4. 789 =   **D.** 348 =

5. 402 =   **E.** 467 =

6. 76 =   **F.** 710 =

TRIPLE MATCH Challenge

Round the product of 40 and 7 to the nearest hundred. _____
Circle the answers that match above.

Solve & Match Math Practice Pages: Grades 2–3 © 2011 Eric Charlesworth, Scholastic Teaching Resources

Name _____   Date _____

Rounding to Thousands

Round each value to the nearest thousand. Draw a line to match each answer on the left with one on the right.

<table>
<tr><td>LEFT</td><td>RIGHT</td></tr>
<tr><td>1. 7,433 =</td><td>A. 4,213 =</td></tr>
<tr><td>2. 3,860 =</td><td>B. 1,500 =</td></tr>
<tr><td>3. 4,560 =</td><td>C. 7,777 =</td></tr>
<tr><td>4. 2,087 =</td><td>D. 7,477 =</td></tr>
<tr><td>5. 7,500 =</td><td>E. 8,745 =</td></tr>
<tr><td>6. 9,350 =</td><td>F. 5,200 =</td></tr>
</table>

TRIPLE MATCH Challenge

Round the product of 300 and 8 to the nearest thousand. _____

Circle the answers that match above.

Solve & Match Math Practice Pages: Grades 2–3 © 2011 Eric Charlesworth, Scholastic Teaching Resources

Name _____ Date _____

Adding 2-Digit Numbers I

Solve each problem. Draw a line to match each sum on the left with one on the right.

LEFT   **RIGHT**

1. 35 + 14 =   **A.** 60 + 29 =

2. 77 + 12 =   **B.** 25 + 24 =

3. 40 + 25 =   **C.** 46 + 22 =

4. 56 + 43 =   **D.** 20 + 25 =

5. 36 + 32 =   **E.** 51 + 14 =

6. 33 + 12 =   **F.** 31 + 68 =

TRIPLE MATCH Challenge

What is the sum of 10, 12, 13 and 14? _____

Circle the answers that match above.

Solve & Match Math Practice Pages: Grades 2–3 © 2011 Eric Charlesworth, Scholastic Teaching Resources

Name _____ Date _____

Adding 2-Digit Numbers II

Solve each problem. Draw a line to match each sum on the left with one on the right.

LEFT   **RIGHT**

1. 45 + 42 =   **A.** 40 + 45 =

2. 18 + 11 =   **B.** 31 + 24 =

3. 57 + 11 =   **C.** 36 + 30 =

4. 33 + 52 =   **D.** 38 + 30 =

5. 41 + 14 =   **E.** 14 + 15 =

6. 44 + 22 =   **F.** 11 + 76 =

TRIPLE MATCH Challenge

In her first basketball game, Anne scored 31 points. In her second game, she scored 24 points. How many total points did she score in the two games? _____

Circle the answers that match above.

Name _____   Date _____

Adding 2-Digit Numbers III: Regrouping

Solve each problem. Draw a line to match each sum on the left with one on the right.

LEFT

1. 29 + 21 =

2. 19 + 11 =

3. 19 + 17 =

4. 39 + 8 =

5. 29 + 28 =

6. 24 + 17 =

RIGHT

A. 38 + 19 =

B. 36 + 14 =

C. 18 + 12 =

D. 18 + 18 =

E. 28 + 13 =

F. 28 + 19 =

TRIPLE MATCH Challenge

Karla was selling candy to raise money for a field trip. In April she sold 22 candy bars and in May she sold 28 candy bars. How many did she sell in total? _____

Circle the answers that match above.

Solve & Match Math Practice Pages: Grades 2–3 © 2011 Eric Charlesworth, Scholastic Teaching Resources

Name _____ Date _____

Adding 2-Digit Numbers IV: Regrouping

Solve each problem. Draw a line to match each sum on the left with one on the right.

LEFT	RIGHT
1. $24 + 67 =$	**A.** $45 + 46 =$
2. $59 + 55 =$	**B.** $79 + 15 =$
3. $67 + 27 =$	**C.** $67 + 17 =$
4. $59 + 25 =$	**D.** $22 + 79 =$
5. $94 + 17 =$	**E.** $99 + 12 =$
6. $32 + 69 =$	**F.** $88 + 26 =$

TRIPLE MATCH Challenge

What sum do you get when you add up 14, 27, 31, and 19? ____
Circle the answers that match above.

Name _____   Date _____

Adding Three Addends: 1-Digit Numbers

Solve each problem. Draw a line to match each sum on the left with one on the right.

LEFT	RIGHT
1. $9 + 7 + 5 =$	**A.** $5 + 5 + 5 =$
2. $9 + 8 + 3 =$	**B.** $9 + 6 + 1 =$
3. $1 + 8 + 7 =$	**C.** $8 + 5 + 7 =$
4. $4 + 3 + 8 =$	**D.** $9 + 9 + 3 =$
5. $8 + 7 + 8 =$	**E.** $7 + 2 + 2 =$
6. $2 + 4 + 5 =$	**F.** $8 + 9 + 6 =$

TRIPLE MATCH Challenge

Lisa had 8 yellow rubber bands, 9 orange ones, and 6 green ones. How many rubber bands did she have in all?

_____

Circle the answers that match above.

Solve & Match Math Practice Pages: Grades 2–3 © 2011 Eric Charlesworth, Scholastic Teaching Resources

Name _____   Date _____

Adding Three Addends: 2-Digit Numbers

Solve each problem. Draw a line to match each sum on the left with one on the right.

LEFT	**RIGHT**
1. $14 + 24 + 34 =$	**A.** $55 + 15 + 29 =$
2. $19 + 18 + 10 =$	**B.** $35 + 25 + 12 =$
3. $22 + 66 + 11 =$	**C.** $23 + 14 + 10 =$
4. $26 + 14 + 13 =$	**D.** $29 + 11 + 22 =$
5. $12 + 21 + 30 =$	**E.** $15 + 30 + 18 =$
6. $20 + 20 + 22 =$	**F.** $30 + 10 + 13 =$

TRIPLE MATCH Challenge

Bart delivered three boxes to the music store. Each box had 21 MP3 players in it. How many MP3 players did he deliver in total? _____

Circle the answers that match above.

Name _____   Date _____

Adding With Multiples of 10

Solve each problem. Draw a line to match each sum on the left with one on the right.

LEFT

RIGHT

1. 90 + 60 =

A. 130 + 130 =

2. 40 + 120 =

B. 70 + 80 =

3. 130 + 130 =

C. 100 + 90 =

4. 20 + 160 =

D. 220 + 120 =

5. 210 + 130 =

E. 170 + 10 =

6. 80 + 110 =

F. 110 + 50 =

TRIPLE MATCH Challenge

Adrian waters plants for his neighbors. This spring he made 100 dollars and in the summer he made 160 dollars. How much money did he make in total? _____

Circle the answers that match above.

Solve & Match Math Practice Pages: Grades 2–3 © 2011 Eric Charlesworth, Scholastic Teaching Resources

Name _____   Date _____

Adding With Multiples of 100

Solve each problem. Draw a line to match each sum on the left with one on the right.

LEFT   **RIGHT**

1. 400 + 700 =   **A.** 600 + 600 =

2. 800 + 900 =   **B.** 300 + 600 =

3. 300 + 900 =   **C.** 1,000 + 700 =

4. 700 + 700 =   **D.** 900 + 500 =

5. 700 + 900 =   **E.** 800 + 800 =

6. 100 + 800 =   **F.** 700 + 400 =

TRIPLE MATCH Challenge

The water park had 500 visitors on Saturday, 400 on Sunday, and 200 on Monday. In total, how many visitors came during that time period? _____

Circle the answers that match above.

Name _____   Date _____

Finding Missing Addends: 1-Digit Numbers

Find the missing addend. Draw a line to match each answer on the left with one on the right.

LEFT

RIGHT

1. ___ + 8 = 14

A. 9 + ___ = 15

2. ___ + 7 = 15

B. 3 + ___ = 11

3. ___ + 3 = 7

C. 2 + ___ = 11

4. ___ + 9 = 14

D. 9 + ___ = 14

5. ___ + 10 = 19

E. 7 + ___ = 14

6. ___ + 3 = 10

F. 10 + ___ = 14

TRIPLE MATCH Challenge

Cindy and Emily have 16 bracelets in total. If Cindy has 9 bracelets, then how many does Emily have? _____

Circle the answers that match above.

Solve & Match Math Practice Pages: Grades 2–3 © 2011 Eric Charlesworth, Scholastic Teaching Resources

Name _____ Date _____

Finding Missing Addends: 2-Digit Numbers

Find the missing addend. Draw a line to match each answer on the left with one on the right.

LEFT

1. ___ + 28 = 43

2. ___ + 17 = 30

3. ___ + 11 = 45

4. ___ + 15 = 50

5. ___ + 11 = 25

6. ___ + 23 = 39

RIGHT

A. 22 + ___ = 56

B. 13 + ___ = 29

C. 10 + ___ = 25

D. 13 + ___ = 27

E. 12 + ___ = 47

F. 32 + ___ = 45

TRIPLE MATCH Challenge

Find the missing addend in this equation:

17 + 12 + 10 + ____ = 54

Circle the answers that match above.

Solve & Match Math Practice Pages: Grades 2–3 © 2011 Eric Charlesworth, Scholastic Teaching Resources

Name _____ Date _____

Solving Word Problems: Monkey Business!

Solve each word problem. Draw a line to match each answer on the left with one on the right. (NOTE: Only the numbers have to match.)

LEFT

1. Deon went to the zoo and saw 4 snub-nose monkeys, 7 spider monkeys, and 9 owl monkeys. How many monkeys did he see in total? _____

2. He bought a stuffed panda bear for $12, a slice of pizza for $2, and a soda for $1. How much money did he spend?

_____

3. There were 23 sharks in the indoor tank and 18 in an outdoor pool. How many sharks were there at the zoo?

_____

4. The zoo had 700 visitors on Saturday and 400 visitors on Sunday. How many visitors did it have that weekend in total?

_____

RIGHT

A. There were three seals that each were fed five fish. How many fish did they eat in all?

_____

B. The concession stand made $600 selling food, $200 selling drinks, and $300 selling stuffed animals. How much money did it make in total?

_____

C. Deon took 20 pictures before lunch and 21 pictures after lunch. How many pictures did he take in all? _____

D. On his last visit, Deon counted 14 emperor penguins. But on this visit there were 6 more. How many emperor penguins were there this time?

_____

Solve & Match Math Practice Pages: Grades 2–3 © 2011 Eric Charlesworth, Scholastic Teaching Resources

Name _____   Date _____

Subtracting 2-Digit Numbers I

Solve each problem. Draw a line to match each difference on the left with one on the right.

LEFT	RIGHT
1. $17 - 12 =$	**A.** $34 - 13 =$
2. $24 - 11 =$	**B.** $39 - 26 =$
3. $96 - 43 =$	**C.** $77 - 40 =$
4. $67 - 30 =$	**D.** $38 - 33 =$
5. $32 - 11 =$	**E.** $79 - 35 =$
6. $58 - 14 =$	**F.** $73 - 20 =$

TRIPLE MATCH Challenge

Randy had 42 beach stones before he collected 14 more. If he gives 12 to his friend, how many will he have left? _____

Circle the answers that match above.

Name _____   Date _____

Subtracting 2-Digit Numbers II

Solve each problem. Draw a line to match each difference on the left with one on the right.

LEFT	**RIGHT**
1. $91 - 40 =$	**A.** $52 - 21 =$
2. $83 - 31 =$	**B.** $95 - 30 =$
3. $47 - 13 =$	**C.** $68 - 34 =$
4. $59 - 28 =$	**D.** $66 - 14 =$
5. $75 - 30 =$	**E.** $67 - 22 =$
6. $87 - 22 =$	**F.** $92 - 41 =$

TRIPLE MATCH Challenge

Fill in the blank: $75 - $ _____ $= 44$

Circle the answers that match above.

Solve & Match Math Practice Pages: Grades 2–3 © 2011 Eric Charlesworth, Scholastic Teaching Resources

Name _____ Date _____

Subtracting 2-Digit Numbers III: Regrouping

Solve each problem. Draw a line to match each difference on the left with one on the right.

LEFT	RIGHT
1. $72 - 17 =$	**A.** $31 - 13 =$
2. $53 - 19 =$	**B.** $73 - 39 =$
3. $60 - 46 =$	**C.** $93 - 27 =$
4. $47 - 29 =$	**D.** $90 - 45 =$
5. $84 - 39 =$	**E.** $93 - 38 =$
6. $80 - 14 =$	**F.** $30 - 16 =$

TRIPLE MATCH Challenge

$$96 - 34 - 21 - 23 = \rule{2cm}{0.4pt}$$

Circle the answers that match above.

Name _____   Date _____

Subtracting 2-Digit Numbers IV: Regrouping

Solve each problem. Draw a line to match each difference on the left with one on the right.

LEFT

1. $98 - 39 =$

2. $44 - 7 =$

3. $78 - 59 =$

4. $56 - 28 =$

5. $63 - 38 =$

6. $24 - 16 =$

RIGHT

A. $30 - 22 =$

B. $50 - 13 =$

C. $73 - 54 =$

D. $61 - 36 =$

E. $77 - 49 =$

F. $64 - 5 =$

TRIPLE MATCH Challenge

The radio station 99.5 MATH plays rap and rock music. On Tuesday afternoon it played 58 songs. If 39 of them were rock songs, how many of them were rap songs? _____

Circle the answers that match above.

Solve & Match Math Practice Pages: Grades 2–3 © 2011 Eric Charlesworth, Scholastic Teaching Resources

Name _____   Date _____

Solving Word Problems: Crazy Camping!

Solve each word problem. Draw a line to match each answer on the left with one on the right. (NOTE: Only the numbers have to match.)

LEFT

1. Ashley and Amber went camping. When Amber went to set up her tent she was missing 11 stakes. If there were supposed to be 30 stakes, how many did she have? _____

2. The camping trip lasted three days, and each day it rained 8 millimeters. How many millimeters did it rain total?

_____

3. They brought a bag of 50 marshmallows, but a raccoon ate 24 of them. How many did the two girls get to eat? _____

4. On the first day, they hiked 4 miles. On each of the next two days, they hiked six miles. How many miles did they hike in total? _____

RIGHT

A. Ashley went canoeing for 46 minutes, but Amber only went for 20 minutes. How many minutes longer did Ashley canoe? _____

B. The temperature was 57 degrees in the afternoon, and 33 degrees at midnight. How many degrees did the temperature decrease? _____

C. On the last morning, Amber counted 11 spiders outside the tent, and Ashley found 5 more. How many spiders did they see? _____

D. The girls slept seven hours each of the first two nights. But on the third night, they only slept for five hours. How many hours did they each sleep on the trip? _____

Name _____   Date _____

Multiplying I: 1-12 Facts

Solve each problem. Draw a line to match each product on the left with one on the right.

LEFT	RIGHT
1. $9 \times 4 =$	**A.** $8 \times 5 =$
2. $8 \times 6 =$	**B.** $6 \times 4 =$
3. $3 \times 8 =$	**C.** $4 \times 4 =$
4. $10 \times 4 =$	**D.** $10 \times 2 =$
5. $2 \times 8 =$	**E.** $12 \times 3 =$
6. $4 \times 5 =$	**F.** $4 \times 12 =$

TRIPLE MATCH Challenge

Mike drove to work and back six days last week. Each day, he had to drive for six miles. How many miles did he drive in total? _____

Circle the answers that match above.

Solve & Match Math Practice Pages: Grades 2–3 © 2011 Eric Charlesworth, Scholastic Teaching Resources

Name _____   Date _____

Multiplying II: 1-12 Facts

Solve each problem. Draw a line to match each product on the left with one on the right.

LEFT

1. $2 \times 12 =$

2. $10 \times 6 =$

3. $4 \times 3 =$

4. $2 \times 9 =$

5. $10 \times 3 =$

6. $6 \times 6 =$

RIGHT

A. $3 \times 8 =$

B. $12 \times 1 =$

C. $6 \times 5 =$

D. $12 \times 5 =$

E. $4 \times 9 =$

F. $6 \times 3 =$

TRIPLE MATCH Challenge

June runs 3 miles each morning and 2 miles every afternoon. How many miles does she run in 12 days? _____

Circle the answers that match above.

Name _____   Date _____

Multiplying III: 1-12 Facts

Solve each problem. Draw a line to match each product on the left with one on the right.

LEFT	RIGHT
1. 9×7	**A.** 3 less than 9×5
2. 6×7	**B.** 3 less than 6×5
3. 5×5	**C.** 4 greater than 7×3
4. 9×6	**D.** 4 less than 8×4
5. 4×7	**E.** 3 greater than 10×6
6. 3×9	**F.** 4 greater than 5×10

TRIPLE MATCH Challenge

Anna went to the shop, where she spent 6 nickels, 2 dimes, and 4 pennies. How many cents did she spend in all? _____

Circle the answers that match above.

Solve & Match Math Practice Pages: Grades 2–3 © 2011 Eric Charlesworth, Scholastic Teaching Resources

Name _____   Date _____

Multiplying IV: 1-12 Facts

Solve each problem. Draw a line to match each product on the left with one on the right.

LEFT   **RIGHT**

1. $8 \times 7 =$ **A.** 40 greater than $8 \times 3 =$

2. $9 \times 8 =$ **B.** 8 less than $10 \times 8 =$

3. $11 \times 4 =$ **C.** 2 greater than $7 \times 6 =$

4. $7 \times 7 =$ **D.** 2 greater than $6 \times 9 =$

5. $8 \times 8 =$ **E.** 60 greater than $7 \times 3 =$

6. $9 \times 9 =$ **F.** 5 less than $9 \times 6 =$

TRIPLE MATCH Challenge

Find the sum of 4 and 6. Multiply that number by 5. Now subtract 1. What number did you end up with? _____

Circle the answers that match above.

Name _____ Date _____

Multiplying With Multiples of 10

Solve each problem. Draw a line to match each product on the left with one on the right.

LEFT	RIGHT
1. $30 \times 4 =$	**A.** $30 \times 2 =$
2. $60 \times 4 =$	**B.** $60 \times 2 =$
3. $50 \times 6 =$	**C.** $80 \times 3 =$
4. $20 \times 3 =$	**D.** $40 \times 4 =$
5. $40 \times 10 =$	**E.** $80 \times 5 =$
6. $80 \times 2 =$	**F.** $30 \times 10 =$

TRIPLE MATCH Challenge

Sam's Market received 12 crates of bread. Each crate had 10 loaves in it. How many loaves of bread did Sam's get in total?

_____

Circle the answers that match above.

Solve & Match Math Practice Pages: Grades 2–3 © 2011 Eric Charlesworth, Scholastic Teaching Resources

Name _____ Date _____

Multiplying With Multiples of 100

Solve each problem. Draw a line to match each product on the left with one on the right.

LEFT	**RIGHT**
1. $400 \times 5 =$	**A.** $1{,}000 \times 2 =$
2. $400 \times 9 =$	**B.** $300 \times 2 =$
3. $300 \times 6 =$	**C.** $600 \times 6 =$
4. $700 \times 5 =$	**D.** $200 \times 5 =$
5. $500 \times 2 =$	**E.** $500 \times 7 =$
6. $100 \times 6 =$	**F.** $900 \times 2 =$

TRIPLE MATCH Challenge

Find the difference of 14 and 9. Now multiply that number by 400. What's your answer? _____

Circle the answers that match above.

Name _____   Date _____

Multiplying With Three Factors I

Solve each problem. Draw a line to match each product on the left with one on the right.

LEFT

1. $4 \times 3 \times 2 =$

2. $2 \times 2 \times 8 =$

3. $3 \times 4 \times 5 =$

4. $3 \times 2 \times 6 =$

5. $3 \times 2 \times 9 =$

6. $1 \times 5 \times 6 =$

RIGHT

A. $2 \times 2 \times 9 =$

B. $12 \times 1 \times 2 =$

C. $3 \times 5 \times 2 =$

D. $2 \times 3 \times 9 =$

E. $4 \times 2 \times 4 =$

F. $3 \times 2 \times 10 =$

TRIPLE MATCH Challenge

What is $2 \times 2 \times 2 \times 2 \times 2$? _____

Circle the answers that match above.

Solve & Match Math Practice Pages: Grades 2–3 © 2011 Eric Charlesworth, Scholastic Teaching Resources

Name _____   Date _____

Multiplying With Three Factors II

Solve each problem. Draw a line to match each product on the left with one on the right.

LEFT

RIGHT

1. $2 \times 2 \times 10 =$

A. $2 \times 5 \times 5 =$

2. $3 \times 3 \times 3 =$

B. $9 \times 1 \times 3 =$

3. $5 \times 2 \times 5 =$

C. $2 \times 4 \times 9 =$

4. $1 \times 3 \times 4 =$

D. $2 \times 2 \times 12 =$

5. $2 \times 3 \times 12 =$

E. $2 \times 2 \times 3 =$

6. $4 \times 2 \times 6 =$

F. $2 \times 4 \times 5 =$

TRIPLE MATCH **Challenge**

Bill has two cages. Each cage contains three spiders. Each spider has eight legs. How many spider legs are there in all?

_____

Circle the answers that match above.

Name _____ Date _____

Solving Word Problems: The School Scene!

Solve each word problem. Draw a line to match each answer on the left with one on the right. (NOTE: Only the numbers have to match.)

LEFT

1. There are nine students in Jane's math group. Each student has three sharpened pencils. How many pencils do they have in all? _____

2. In PE class, Jane was playing basketball. She scored five 2-point baskets and three 3-point baskets. How many points did she score? _____

3. In art class, there were six students who made paper-clip sculptures. Each student used 12 paper clips. How many paper clips were used in total? _____

4. In language arts, Jane read 3 pages from each of 8 different magazines. How many pages did she read in all? _____

RIGHT

A. In social studies, the class was divided into six groups with four students in each group. How many students are in the class? _____

B. There are nine rows of lockers, and each row has eight lockers. How many lockers are there in total? _____

C. At lunch, the cafeteria started with 30 turkey sandwiches. After 11 students had picked turkey sandwiches, how many were left? _____

D. Jane is nine years old. Her teacher, Ms. Wohl, is three times as old as she is. How old is Ms. Wohl? _____

Solve & Match Math Practice Pages: Grades 2–3 © 2011 Eric Charlesworth, Scholastic Teaching Resources

Name _____   Date _____

Dividing I: 1-12 Facts

Solve each problem. Draw a line to match each quotient on the left with one on the right.

LEFT   **RIGHT**

1. $54 \div 9 =$ **A.** $70 \div 7 =$

2. $12 \div 4 =$ **B.** $21 \div 7 =$

3. $24 \div 6 =$ **C.** $4 \div 4 =$

4. $36 \div 3 =$ **D.** $12 \div 2 =$

5. $40 \div 4 =$ **E.** $24 \div 2 =$

6. $7 \div 7 =$ **F.** $36 \div 9 =$

TRIPLE MATCH Challenge

Cindy wants to read 36 books this year. Since there are 12 months in a year, she is trying to figure out how many books she needs to read per month. What's her answer? _____

Circle the answers that match above.

Solve & Match Math Practice Pages: Grades 2–3 © 2011 Eric Charlesworth, Scholastic Teaching Resources

Name _____   Date _____

Dividing II: 1-12 Facts

Solve each problem. Draw a line to match each quotient on the left with one on the right.

LEFT	RIGHT
1. $24 \div 3 =$	**A.** $4 \div 1 =$
2. $77 \div 7 =$	**B.** $25 \div 5 =$
3. $30 \div 10 =$	**C.** $72 \div 9 =$
4. $42 \div 6 =$	**D.** $33 \div 3 =$
5. $48 \div 12 =$	**E.** $9 \div 3 =$
6. $10 \div 2 =$	**F.** $49 \div 7 =$

TRIPLE MATCH Challenge

Three brothers each have the same number of video games. If they have 21 games in all, how many does each brother have?

_____

Circle the answers that match above.

Solve & Match Math Practice Pages: Grades 2–3 © 2011 Eric Charlesworth, Scholastic Teaching Resources

Name _____ Date _____

Dividing III: 1-12 Facts

Solve each problem. Draw a line to match each quotient on the left with one on the right.

LEFT	RIGHT
1. $30 \div 6 =$	**A.** $24 \div 3 =$
2. $6 \div 2 =$	**B.** $24 \div 8 =$
3. $56 \div 8 =$	**C.** $28 \div 4 =$
4. $36 \div 6 =$	**D.** $18 \div 3 =$
5. $48 \div 6 =$	**E.** $40 \div 10 =$
6. $16 \div 4 =$	**F.** $45 \div 9 =$

TRIPLE MATCH Challenge

Luna's apartment building has six floors and 24 apartments. If each floor has the same number of apartments, how many are on each floor? _____

Circle the answers that match above.

Name _____   Date _____

Dividing IV: 1-12 Facts

Solve each problem. Draw a line to match each quotient on the left with one on the right.

LEFT	RIGHT
1. $63 \div 7 =$	**A.** $12 \div 1 =$
2. $63 \div 9 =$	**B.** $35 \div 7 =$
3. $20 \div 2 =$	**C.** $33 \div 11 =$
4. $27 \div 9 =$	**D.** $18 \div 2 =$
5. $25 \div 5 =$	**E.** $80 \div 8 =$
6. $72 \div 6 =$	**F.** $56 \div 8 =$

TRIPLE MATCH Challenge

Fill in the blank. $50 \div \underline{\quad} = 5$.

Circle the answers that match above.

Solve & Match Math Practice Pages: Grades 2–3 © 2011 Eric Charlesworth, Scholastic Teaching Resources

Name _____   Date _____

Solving Word Problems: Food Frenzy!

Solve each word problem. Draw a line to match each answer on the left with one on the right. (NOTE: Only the numbers have to match.)

LEFT

1. After a great win, Jeanette's soccer team went out to eat. There were nine people and they ordered 27 slices of pizza. If everyone had the same number of slices, how many did they each eat? _____

2. Five teammates equally shared a plate of 30 mozzarella sticks. How many did they each eat?
_____

3. Each of the eight people drank eight ounces of water. How many ounces did they drink in all? _____

4. The waiter brought 20 slices of bread to the table, and the team ate 13 of them. How many were left? _____

RIGHT

A. Four teammates got ice cream for dessert. If they shared 12 scoops equally, how many scoops did each player eat?
_____

B. Jeanette was served a plate with 38 french fries. She ate 31 of them and gave the rest to Mark. How many did Mark get?
_____

C. Each of the two coaches paid $32 for the meal. How much was the total cost? _____

D. At first, the coaches gave $70 to pay for the meal. How much change did they get back?
_____

Name _____   Date _____

Adding Coins I

Add the coins in each picture. Draw a line to match each sum
on the left with one on the right.

LEFT   **RIGHT**

1. =

A. =

2. =

B. =

3. =

C. =

4. =

D. =

5. =

E. =

6. =

F. =

TRIPLE MATCH Challenge

Rachel bought a pack of gum. She paid with a dollar and
received two quarters and a nickel in change. How much did
the gum cost? _____

Circle the answers that match above.

Solve & Match Math Practice Pages: Grades 2–3 © 2011 Eric Charlesworth, Scholastic Teaching Resources

Name _____ Date _____

Adding Coins II

Add the coins in each picture. Draw a line to match each sum on the left with one on the right.

LEFT   **RIGHT**

1.  =   A.  =

2. =   B. =

3. =   C. =

4. =   D. =

5. =   E. =

6. =   F. =

TRIPLE MATCH Challenge

If Percy had one more dime, he would have a dollar. How much money does he have? _____

Circle the answers that match above.

Solve & Match Math Practice Pages: Grades 2–3 © 2011 Eric Charlesworth, Scholastic Teaching Resources

Name _____   Date _____

Solving Word Problems: Shopping Spree!

Solve each word problem. Draw a line to match each answer on the left with one on the right. (NOTE: Only the numbers have to match.)

LEFT

1. Isabel bought 20 more pens than Natalie did. If Natalie, bought 10 pens, how many pens did Isabel buy? _____

2. Ariel bought a baseball bat for $19, a hat for $21, and a ball for $4. Out of those items, what was the highest price? _____

3. Jessica spent two quarters, six nickels, and six pennies. How much money is that? _____

4. Nick spent 40 cents less than Jessica did. How much did he spend? _____

RIGHT

A. Steve bought sneakers for $49, a coat for $86, and a pair of pants for $22. What was the highest price of those items? _____

B. Cole's sneakers cost $3 less than the sneakers Steve bought. How much did they cost? _____

C. Genesis bought two candies that each cost a dime. She also bought a gumball for one penny. How much did she spend? _____

D. Kassielle counted her change and had two dimes, a nickel, and five pennies. How much money did she have left? _____

Solve & Match Math Practice Pages: Grades 2–3 © 2011 Eric Charlesworth, Scholastic Teaching Resources

Name _____   Date _____

Solving for Elapsed Time: Hours

Match each time on the left with the correct clock on the right.

LEFT   **RIGHT**

1. Fours hours after 6:00 =   **A.**  =

2. Two hours after 2:00 =   **B.** =

3. Two hours before 2:00 =   **C.** =

4. Seven hours after 1:00 =   **D.** =

5. One hour before 7:00 =   **E.** =

6. Six hours after 3:00 =   **F.** =

TRIPLE MATCH Challenge

Shaniel went to the beach at 10:00 AM and stayed for six hours. What time did he leave the beach? _____

Circle the answers that match above.

Name _____   Date _____

Solving for Elapsed Time: Hours & Half-Hours

Match each time on the left with the correct clock on the right.

LEFT

1. 3 hours before 5:30 =

2. $3\frac{1}{2}$ hours after 7:00 =

3. 6 hours after 6:00 =

4. $1\frac{1}{2}$ hours before 9:30 =

5. 10 hours before 12:00 =

6. $5\frac{1}{2}$ hours after 3:00 =

RIGHT

A. =

B. =

C. =

D. =

E. =

F. =

TRIPLE MATCH Challenge

Dave went for a run. He left at 6:00 and ran 12 miles. If he ran 6 miles each hour, at what time did he stop running? _____

Circle the answers that match above.

Solve & Match Math Practice Pages: Grades 2–3 © 2011 Eric Charlesworth, Scholastic Teaching Resources

Name _____   Date _____

Solving for Elapsed Time: Hours & Minutes

Match each time on the left with the correct clock on the right.

LEFT   **RIGHT**

1. One hour and 15 minutes after 7:00 =

    A.  =

2. Three hours and 20 minutes after 1:00 =

    B. =

3. 45 minutes before 8:00 =

    C. =

4. Six hours and 45 minutes before 8:00 =

    D. =

5. One hour and 10 minutes before 4:00 =

    E. =

6. 55 minutes after 12:00 =

    F. =

TRIPLE MATCH Challenge

Theo started surfing at 5:30. He surfed for one hour and 45 minutes. What time did he finish surfing? _____

Circle the answers that match above.

Name _____ Date _____

Converting Units: Weeks & Days

Find the total number of **days**. Draw a line to match each answer on the left with one on the right.

LEFT	RIGHT
1. 2 weeks and 5 days =	**A.** 4 weeks and 12 days =
2. 6 weeks =	**B.** 5 weeks and 7 days =
3. 4 weeks and 1 day =	**C.** 2 weeks and 15 days =
4. 3 weeks and 9 days =	**D.** 4 weeks and 2 days =
5. 5 weeks and 5 days =	**E.** 3 weeks and 7 days =
6. 4 weeks =	**F.** 1 week and 12 days =

TRIPLE MATCH Challenge

Rob is going on a camping trip for two days LESS than three weeks. For how many days will he be camping? _____

Circle the answers that match above.

Solve & Match Math Practice Pages: Grades 2–3 © 2011 Eric Charlesworth, Scholastic Teaching Resources

Name _____ Date _____

Converting Units: Feet & Inches

Find the total number of **inches**. Draw a line to match each answer on the left with one on the right.

LEFT	**RIGHT**
1. 3 feet and 12 inches =	**A.** 2 feet and 8 inches =
2. 5 feet =	**B.** 4 feet =
3. 1 foot and 14 inches =	**C.** 2 feet and 12 inches =
4. 1 foot and 20 inches =	**D.** 6 feet and 25 inches =
5. 3 feet =	**E.** 2 feet and 2 inches =
6. 8 feet and 1 inch =	**F.** 4 feet and 12 inches =

TRIPLE MATCH Challenge

Zora threw a ball that flew for three feet in the air before rolling another two feet on the ground. How many inches did the ball travel in all? _____

Circle the answers that match above.

Name _____   Date _____

Finding Perimeter

Find the perimeter of each shape. Draw a line to match each answer on the left with one on the right.

LEFT   **RIGHT**

1. 3 5 9 _____   **A.** 5 5 5 5 _____

2. 7 7 7 7 _____   **B.** 2 7 2 7 _____

3. 6 3 3 6 _____   **C.** 5 12 11 _____

4. 4 3 5 8 _____   **D.** 2 6 3 6 _____

TRIPLE MATCH Challenge

There is an equilateral triangle in which all sides are 6. What is the perimeter of the triangle? _____

Circle the answers that match above.

Solve & Match Math Practice Pages: Grades 2–3 © 2011 Eric Charlesworth, Scholastic Teaching Resources

Name _____ Date _____

Find the Missing Side

Find the length of the missing side. Draw a line to match each answer on the left with one on the right.

LEFT   **RIGHT**

1.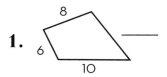
8
6
10
Perimeter = 33

A.
2
8
6
8
Perimeter = 29

2.
5   5
5
5
Perimeter = 25

B.
11
11
Perimeter = 33

3.
7
10
Perimeter = 27

C.
9
9
9
Perimeter = 36

4.
4
3
12
Perimeter = 30

D.
5
11
Perimeter = 26

TRIPLE MATCH Challenge

A regular hexagon has six equal sides. If the perimeter of a regular hexagon is 66, what is the length of each side? _____

Circle the answers that match above.

Name _____   Date _____

Finding the Area of Rectangles

Find the area of each rectangle. Draw a line to match each answer on the left with one on the right.

LEFT   **RIGHT**

1. 4 ⬜ (6)

Area = _____

A. 3 ⬜ (3)

Area = _____

2. 2 ▭ (8)

Area = _____

B. 3 ▭ (8)

Area = _____

3. 1 ▭ (9)

Area = _____

C. 4 ⬜ (4)

Area = _____

4. 2 ▭ (9)

Area = _____

D. 6 ▯ (3)

Area = _____

TRIPLE MATCH Challenge

A square has a perimeter of 16. What is the area of the square?

_____

Circle the answers that match above.

Solve & Match Math Practice Pages: Grades 2–3 © 2011 Eric Charlesworth, Scholastic Teaching Resources

Name _____ Date _____

Solving Word Problems:
In the Construction Zone!

Solve each word problem. Draw a line to match each answer on the left with one on the right. (NOTE: Only the numbers have to match.)

LEFT

1. Federal builders are constructing a hotel that will have eight floors. Each floor will have five rooms. How many rooms will there be in all?

   _____

2. The pool is the shape of a square. Each side has a length of 12 meters. What is the perimeter of the pool? _____

3. What is the area of the pool?

   _____

4. The shallow end of the pool is 3 feet, 9 inches deep. How many inches deep is it? _____

RIGHT

A. The construction crew has 12 trucks. Each truck has four wheels. How many wheels are there at the site? _____

B. They have worked on the site for 20 weeks and 4 days. How many days have they been working? _____

C. The height of the building will be 150 feet. Right now it is 105 feet. How many more feet need to be added to the top?

   _____

D. Ted worked at the site for four days. If he worked for ten hours each day, how many total hours did he work in total? _____

Name _____   Date _____

Identifying Fractions

Write the fraction shown. Put each answer in simplest form. Draw a line to match each answer on the left with one on the right.

LEFT   **RIGHT**

1. _____   A. _____

2.   _____   B. _____

3.   _____   C. _____

4. _____   D. _____

5. _____   E. _____

6. _____   F. _____

TRIPLE MATCH Challenge

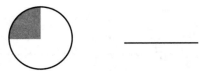

Eliza ordered a whole pizza and ate one-fourth of it. What fraction of the pizza was left? _____

Circle the answers that match above.

Solve & Match Math Practice Pages: Grades 2–3 © 2011 Eric Charlesworth, Scholastic Teaching Resources

Name _____   Date _____

Adding Like Fractions

Find each sum. Draw a line to match each sum on the left with one on the right.

LEFT

RIGHT

1. $\frac{1}{10} + \frac{5}{10} =$

A. $\frac{4}{10} + \frac{1}{10} =$

2. $\frac{1}{6} + \frac{3}{6} =$

B. $\frac{2}{5} + \frac{3}{5} =$

3. $\frac{1}{5} + \frac{3}{5} =$

C. $\frac{2}{6} + \frac{2}{6} =$

4. $\frac{3}{10} + \frac{2}{10} =$

D. $\frac{4}{10} + \frac{2}{10} =$

5. $\frac{5}{12} + \frac{4}{12} =$

E. $\frac{2}{5} + \frac{2}{5} =$

6. $\frac{4}{5} + \frac{1}{5} =$

F. $\frac{7}{12} + \frac{2}{12} =$

TRIPLE MATCH Challenge

Find the sum: $\frac{2}{10} + \frac{2}{10} + \frac{2}{10} =$? _____

Circle the answers that match above.

Name _____   Date _____

Subtracting Like Fractions

Find each difference. Draw a line to match each difference on the left with one on the right.

LEFT	**RIGHT**
1. $\frac{7}{8} - \frac{3}{8} =$	**A.** $\frac{7}{10} - \frac{1}{10} =$
2. $\frac{2}{4} - \frac{1}{4} =$	**B.** $\frac{5}{8} - \frac{2}{8} =$
3. $\frac{4}{6} - \frac{2}{6} =$	**C.** $\frac{5}{6} - \frac{3}{6} =$
4. $\frac{9}{10} - \frac{3}{10} =$	**D.** $\frac{5}{8} - \frac{1}{8} =$
5. $\frac{5}{6} - \frac{4}{6} =$	**E.** $\frac{2}{6} - \frac{1}{6} =$
6. $\frac{7}{8} - \frac{4}{8} =$	**F.** $\frac{3}{4} - \frac{2}{4} =$

TRIPLE MATCH Challenge

Celine had $\frac{8}{10}$ of a gallon of milk. After she fed her cat $\frac{2}{10}$ of a gallon, what fraction did she have left? _____

Circle the answers that match above.

Solve & Match Math Practice Pages: Grades 2–3 © 2011 Eric Charlesworth, Scholastic Teaching Resources

Name _____   Date _____

Simplifying Fractions

Put each fraction into simplest form. Draw a line to match each answer on the left with one on the right.

LEFT

1. $\frac{4}{6}$ = _____

2. $\frac{2}{6}$ = _____

3. $\frac{4}{8}$ = _____

4. $\frac{6}{8}$ = _____

5. $\frac{16}{20}$ = _____

6. $\frac{3}{12}$ = _____

RIGHT

A. $\frac{2}{8}$ = _____

B. $\frac{8}{10}$ = _____

C. $\frac{9}{12}$ = _____

D. $\frac{2}{4}$ = _____

E. $\frac{3}{9}$ = _____

F. $\frac{6}{9}$ = _____

TRIPLE MATCH Challenge

The fractions $\frac{25}{75}$ and $\frac{100}{300}$ are equivalent. When put in simplest form, what do they equal? _____

Circle the answers that match above.

Name _____ Date _____

Mixed Practice

Solve each problem. Draw a line to match each answer on the left with one on the right.

LEFT

RIGHT

1. $58 - 38 =$

A. What is double the number 5?

2. $4 \times 9 =$

B. $99 - 59 =$

3. $22 + 18 =$

C. What is double the number 10?

4. $60 \div 6 =$

D. $11 \times 5 =$

5. $12 \times 5 =$

E. $6 \times 10 =$

6. $27 + 28 =$

F. How many inches are in 3 feet?

TRIPLE MATCH Challenge

Each side of a triangle measures 40 inches. How many feet is the perimeter of that triangle? _____

Circle the answers that match above.

Solve & Match Math Practice Pages: Grades 2–3 © 2011 Eric Charlesworth, Scholastic Teaching Resources

Answer Key

PAGE 5
1. 10
2. 30
3. 12
4. 5
5. 40
6. 400
A. 12
B. 400
C. 10
D. 5
E. 40
F. 30
TMC: 12

PAGE 6
1. 50
2. 33
3. 4
4. 8
5. 60
6. 3
A. 3
B. 33
C. 60
D. 50
E. 8
F. 4
TMC: 8

PAGE 7
1. 16
2. 2
3. 14
4. 6
5. 15
6. 24
A. 16
B. 14
C. 2
D. 24
E. 15
F. 6
TMC: 15

PAGE 8
1. ten thousands
2. ones
3. thousands
4. hundred thousands
5. tens
6. hundreds
A. ones
B. hundred thousands
C. hundreds
D. tens
E. ten thousands
F. thousands
TMC: hundreds

PAGE 9
1. 117
2. 150
3. 137
4. 191
5. 155
6. 145
A. 150
B. 155
C. 145
D. 117
E. 191
F. 137
TMC: 117

PAGE 10
1. 12
2. 18
3. 24
4. 30
5. 20
6. 6
A. 18
B. 20
C. 12
D. 24
E. 6
F. 30
TMC: 24

PAGE 11
1. 20
2. 30
3. 10
4. 70
5. 50
6. 90
A. 70
B. 90
C. 20
D. 50
E. 10
F. 30
TMC: 70

PAGE 12
1. 700
2. 500
3. 300
4. 800
5. 400
6. 100
A. 100
B. 400
C. 800
D. 300
E. 500
F. 700
TMC: 300

PAGE 13
1. 7,000
2. 4,000
3. 5,000
4. 2,000
5. 8,000
6. 9,000
A. 4,000
B. 2,000
C. 8,000
D. 7,000
E. 9,000
F. 5,000
TMC: 2,000

PAGE 14
1. 49
2. 89
3. 65
4. 99
5. 68
6. 45
A. 89
B. 49
C. 68
D. 45
E. 65
F. 99
TMC: 49

PAGE 15
1. 87
2. 29
3. 68
4. 85
5. 55
6. 66
A. 85
B. 55
C. 66
D. 68
E. 29
F. 87
TMC: 55

PAGE 16
1. 50
2. 30
3. 36
4. 47
5. 57
6. 41
A. 57
B. 50
C. 30
D. 36
E. 41
F. 47
TMC: 50

PAGE 17
1. 91
2. 114
3. 94
4. 84
5. 111
6. 101
A. 91
B. 94
C. 84
D. 101
E. 111
F. 114
TMC: 91

PAGE 18
1. 21
2. 20
3. 16
4. 15
5. 23
6. 11
A. 15
B. 16

C. 20
D. 21
E. 11
F. 23
TMC: 23

PAGE 19
1. 72
2. 47
3. 99
4. 53
5. 63
6. 62
A. 99
B. 72
C. 47
D. 62
E. 63
F. 53
TMC: 63

PAGE 20
1. 150
2. 160
3. 260
4. 180
5. 340
6. 190
A. 260
B. 150
C. 190
D. 340
E. 180
F. 160
TMC: 260

PAGE 21
1. 1,100
2. 1,700
3. 1,200
4. 1,400
5. 1,600
6. 900
A. 1,200
B. 900
C. 1,700
D. 1,400
E. 1,600
F. 1,100
TMC: 1,100

PAGE 22
1. 6
2. 8
3. 4
4. 5
5. 9
6. 7
A. 6
B. 8
C. 9
D. 5
E. 7
F. 4
TMC: 7

PAGE 23
1. 15
2. 13
3. 34
4. 35
5. 14
6. 16
A. 34
B. 16
C. 15
D. 14
E. 35
F. 13
TMC: 15

PAGE 24
1. 20
2. 15 dollars
3. 41
4. 1,100
A. 15
B. 1,100
C. 41
D. 20

PAGE 25
1. 5
2. 13
3. 53
4. 37
5. 21
6. 44
A. 21
B. 13
C. 37
D. 5
E. 44
F. 53
TMC: 44

PAGE 26
1. 51
2. 52
3. 34
4. 31
5. 45
6. 65
A. 31
B. 65
C. 34
D. 52
E. 45
F. 51
TMC: 31

PAGE 27
1. 55
2. 34
3. 14
4. 18
5. 45
6. 66
A. 18
B. 34
C. 66
D. 45
E. 55
F. 14
TMC: 18

PAGE 28
1. 59
2. 37
3. 19
4. 28
5. 25
6. 8
A. 8
B. 37
C. 19
D. 25
E. 28
F. 59
TMC: 19

PAGE 29
1. 19
2. 24
3. 26
4. 16
A. 26
B. 24
C. 16
D. 19

PAGE 30
1. 36
2. 48
3. 24
4. 40
5. 16
6. 20
A. 40
B. 24
C. 16
D. 20
E. 36
F. 48
TMC: 36

PAGE 31
1. 24
2. 60
3. 12
4. 18
5. 30
6. 36
A. 24
B. 12
C. 30
D. 60
E. 36
F. 18
TMC: 60

PAGE 32
1. 63
2. 42
3. 25
4. 54
5. 28
6. 27
A. 42
B. 27
C. 25
D. 28
E. 63
F. 54
TMC: 54

PAGE 33
1. 56
2. 72
3. 44
4. 49
5. 64
6. 81
A. 64
B. 72

C. 44
D. 56
E. 81
F. 49
TMC: 49

PAGE 34
1. 120
2. 240
3. 300
4. 60
5. 400
6. 160
A. 60
B. 120
C. 240
D. 160
E. 400
F. 300
TMC: 120

PAGE 35
1. 2,000
2. 3,600
3. 1,800
4. 3,500
5. 1,000
6. 600
A. 2,000
B. 600
C. 3,600
D. 1,000
E. 3,500
F. 1,800
TMC: 2,000

PAGE 36
1. 24
2. 32
3. 60
4. 36
5. 54
6. 30
A. 36
B. 24
C. 30
D. 54
E. 32
F. 60
TMC: 32

PAGE 37
1. 40
2. 27
3. 50
4. 12
5. 72
6. 48
A. 50
B. 27
C. 72
D. 48
E. 12
F. 40
TMC: 48

PAGE 38
1. 27
2. 19
3. 72
4. 24
A. 24
B. 72
C. 19
D. 27

PAGE 39
1. 6
2. 3
3. 4
4. 12
5. 10
6. 1
A. 10
B. 3
C. 1
D. 6
E. 12
F. 4
TMC: 3

PAGE 40
1. 8
2. 11
3. 3
4. 7
5. 4
6. 5
A. 4
B. 5
C. 8
D. 11
E. 3
F. 7
TMC: 7

PAGE 41
1. 5
2. 3
3. 7
4. 6
5. 8
6. 4
A. 8
B. 3
C. 7
D. 6
E. 4
F. 5
TMC: 4

PAGE 42
1. 9
2. 7
3. 10
4. 3
5. 5
6. 12
A. 12
B. 5
C. 3
D. 9
E. 10
F. 7
TMC: 10

PAGE 43
1. 3
2. 6
3. 64
4. 7
A. 3
B. 7
C. 64 dollars
D. 6 dollars

PAGE 44
1. 11
2. 51
3. 45
4. 30
5. 76
6. 50
A. 11
B. 30
C. 51
D. 50
E. 76
F. 45
TMC: 45 cents

PAGE 45
1. 41
2. 30
3. 28
4. 17
5. 35
6. 90
A. 35
B. 90
C. 41
D. 30
E. 17
F. 28
TMC: 90 cents

PAGE 46
1. 30
2. 21 dollars
3. 86 cents
4. 46 cents
A. 86 dollars
B. 46 dollars
C. 21 cents
D. 30 cents

PAGE 47
1. 10:00
2. 4:00
3. 12:00
4. 8:00
5. 6:00
6. 9:00
A. 4:00
B. 6:00
C. 10:00
D. 12:00
E. 8:00
F. 9:00
TMC: 4:00 PM

PAGE 48
1. 2:30
2. 10:30
3. 12:00
4. 8:00
5. 2:00
6. 8:30
A. 12:00
B. 8:30
C. 2:00
D. 10:30
E. 2:30
F. 8:00
TMC: 8:00

PAGE 49
1. 8:15
2. 4:20
3. 7:15
4. 1:15
5. 2:50
6. 12:55
A. 2:50
B. 8:15
C. 12:55
D. 7:15
E. 4:20
F. 1:15
TMC: 7:15

PAGE 50
1. 19
2. 42
3. 29
4. 30
5. 40
6. 28
A. 40
B. 42
C. 29
D. 30
E. 28
F. 19
TMC: 19

PAGE 51
1. 48
2. 60
3. 26
4. 32
5. 36
6. 97
A. 32
B. 48
C. 36
D. 97
E. 26
F. 60
TMC: 60

PAGE 52
1. 17
2. 28
3. 18
4. 20
A. 20
B. 18
C. 28

D. 17
TMC: 18

PAGE 53
1. 9
2. 5
3. 10
4. 11
A. 5
B. 11
C. 9
D. 10
TMC: 11

PAGE 54
1. 24
2. 16
3. 9
4. 18
A. 9
B. 24
C. 16
D. 18
TMC: 16

PAGE 55
1. 40
2. 48 meters
3. 144 meters
4. 45
A. 48
B. 144
C. 45
D. 40

PAGE 56
1. ⅓
2. ½
3. ⅔ (⁸⁄₁₂)
4. ¼
5. ¾
6. ⅙
A. ¾
B. ½ (²⁄₄)
C. ⅙ (²⁄₁₂)
D. ⅔
E. ⅓ (²⁄₆)
F. ¼
TMC: ¾

PAGE 57
1. ⁶⁄₁₀ (⅗)
2. ⁴⁄₆ (⅔)
3. ⅘
4. ⁵⁄₁₀ (½)
5. ⁹⁄₁₂ (¾)
6. ⁵⁄₅ (1)
A. ⁵⁄₁₀ (½)
B. ⁵⁄₅ (1)
C. ⁴⁄₆ (⅔)
D. ⁶⁄₁₀ (⅗)
E. ⅘
F. ⁹⁄₁₂ (¾)
TMC: ⁶⁄₁₀

PAGE 58
1. ⁴⁄₈
2. ¼
3. ²⁄₆
4. ⁶⁄₁₀
5. ⅙
6. ⅜
A. ⁶⁄₁₀
B. ⅜
C. ²⁄₆
D. ⁴⁄₈
E. ⅙
F. ¼
TMC: ⁶⁄₁₀ (⅗)

PAGE 59
1. ⅔
2. ⅓
3. ½
4. ¾
5. ⅘
6. ¼
A. ¼
B. ⅘
C. ¾
D. ½
E. ⅓
F. ⅔
TMC: ⅓

PAGE 60
1. 20
2. 36
3. 40
4. 10
5. 60
6. 55
A. 10

B. 40
C. 20
D. 55
E. 60
F. 36
TMC: 10